Scattered Pearls

By
Shaykh Mufti Saiful Islām

JKN Publications

First Published in August 2015

ISBN 978-1-909114-13-5

British Library Cataloguing in Publication Data
A catalogue record for this book is available from the British Library.

Publisher's Note,

Every care and attention has been put into the production of this book. If however, you find any errors, they are our own, for which we seek Allāh's ﷻ forgiveness and reader's pardon.

Published by,

JKN Publications
118 Manningham Lane
Bradford
West Yorkshire
BD8 7JF
United Kingdom

t, +44 (0) 1274 308 456 | w, www.jkn.org.uk | e, info@jkn.org.uk

Book Title, Scattered Pearls

Author, Shaykh Mufti Saiful Islām

Printed by Mega Printing in Turkey

"In the Name of Allāh, the Most Beneficent,
the Most Merciful"

Contents

Introduction

All Praises be to Allāh ﷻ. Peace and salutations be upon the last of the Messengers ﷺ, our Beloved Prophet Muhammad ﷺ, upon his noble Companions ؓ and upon those who follow their noble life-styles until the final hour.

Today, spreading a message of any kind has become easy and simple by mere click of a button or touch of a screen. Most of us have some sort of access to some form of social media at all times whether it is WhatsApp or face book, twitter to name a few.

However, this faculty of social media is like a double-edged sword; it can either be utilised in a positive or a negative way. We can use it to receive and share messages/information in the form of text, emails, images, audio recordings or videos that will either benefit us in our Deen or can be a means of indulgence in futile or sinful activities. It is therefore down to us as to how we choose to utilise it; whether to benefit us or harm us.

Islamically, there are many benefits of using the social media for the work of Deen such as charity work, Islamic conferences/ programs, talks, publications, all of which can be promoted quickly and effectively.

This book in your hands is a collection of 'scattered pearls' in a book format taken from the social media via magazines, emails and WhatsApp messages. I have mentioned some of the messages sent to me via scholars, friends and colleagues which I thought would be of immense benefit and also interesting for our readers. These pearls will hopefully increase our knowledge and wisdom and most importantly make us realise our purpose of life. May Allāh ﷻ accept this compilation and make it a means of salvation and success in both worlds. Āmeen.

Shaykh Mufti Saiful Islām
Principal of JKN, Bradford
August2015/Dhul-Qa'dah 1436

Social Media and the Internet

The following is a summary of Shaykh Abdur Raheem Sāhib's speech in Masjid Umar, Dewsbury.

Social media is a double sided sword

Advantages,
1) A person could keep contact with his Shaykh, family, relatives etc.
2) One could gain knowledge from correct and authentic sources.

Disadvantages,
This could be broken down into 2 points:

1) Fitnah of Beliefs
Nowadays, we find many flashy websites which attract a lay person but they effect a person's Imān. Many a time because of these websites, a person gets doubts in his Imān and sometimes, he even looses his Imān.

Q: How do we protect our Imān?
A, a) Read reliable books on the topic of Aqāid to increase your knowledge. Keep on studying, do not be satisfied on what you have learned in Maktab.
b) Continuously do good deeds (Salāh, Tilāwah, Zikr etc). Through these A'māl, we can save ourselves from the doubts of Shaytān.

2) Fitnah of A'māl,

a) Social media prevents us from performing Salāh with congregation. Maulāna Saifur Rahmān Sāhib says, "According to my understanding, the worst Fitnah in our times is the mobile phone."

b) Pornography, nudity etc.

This is a very wide spread illness and causes so many fights and divorces in our community. Also, our family life is shattered. Shaykh Yūsuf Darwān Sāhib said, "Our homes have become hotels."

Stay close to the Ulamā and take their advise.

يَآ أَيُّهَا الَّذِينَ آمَنُوٓا أَطِيعُوا اللهَ وَأَطِيعُوا الرَّسُولَ وَأُولِي الْأَمْرِ مِنْكُمْ

O Believers! Obey Allah and obey the Messenger and those in authorities (scholars) amongst you. (4:59)

Etiquettes of using social media

1) Taqwa- constant awareness of Allāh ﷻ.

2) Say Bismillāh before opening your phone, computer etc.

3) Correct your intention before using and if for some reason Shaytān instigates you, stop yourself.

4) If you happen to make a mistake, repent immediately and whenever you do a mistake, keep doing Tawbah; a day will come that this continuous Tawbah will stop you from sins.

5) Do not waste time on the internet. Wasting time is harmful for your spiritual health and also your physical health.

وَالْعَصْرِ ٥ إِنَّ الْإِنْسَانَ لَفِي خُسْرٍ

By the oath of time. Verily mankind is at a loss. (103:1-2)

Allāh ﷻ takes oath of time to show the importance of it.

Shaykh Ruknuddin, Khaleefah of Khwāja Bahāuddeen Zakariyyā Multāni ﷺ says,

Janābah of the body is by going to the wife.
Janābah of the heart is by evil company.

The body is cleansed by water.
The heart should be cleansed by the company of the Sāliheen (pious people).

May Allāh ﷻ have mercy upon the Ummah and guide us towards the Haqq (truth). May Allāh ﷻ help the Muslim Ummah and elevate the Kalimah throughout the world. Āmeen.

Our Pious Predecessors' Love For Sunnah

Shaykhul Hind Maulāna Mahmoodul Hasan Sāhib ﷺ was a great saint and scholar of his time. He would tend to his Qurbāni cow for the entire year. He would personally wash and feed the animal.

10

The cow would also become very attached to him. When he would leave his home to deliver the lessons of Saheeh Bukhāri and other books of Hadeeth at Dārul 'Uloom Deoband, it would follow him right to the Madrasah gate where it would sit down. When he would return at noon after lessons, it would follow him back home.

When the days of Qurbāni drew near, he would lessen its normal feed, which was grass, and substitute it with bucketful of milk and jalebi (sweet). He would also apply mendhi (henna) to it, place flowers on its back and beautify it because Allāh 🙰 commands that one's most beloved wealth should be spent in the path of Allāh 🙰. Thus, he would begin to love the animal very deeply. After the 'Eidul Adha Salāh, he would sacrifice it and cry a little as well. Then he would immediately purchase another cow for the following 'Eid. *(Maslak-e-Ulama-e-Deoband aur Hubbe Rasūl)*

Once he kept a cow which he fed the entire year. He would take it to the jungle after Asr Salāh and make it run in order to make it healthy. It became so healthy that he received offers of up to 80 rupees for it whereas, a healthy cow in those days would cost approximately 10 to 15 rupees. However, he did not accept any offer. *(Khutubāte Hakeemul Ummat, vol. 17, pg. 154)*

Since it was his habit to offer a few Qurbāni every year, he desired to do the same while he was imprisoned at Malta. Though prisoners are not allowed to slaughter, he nevertheless forwarded the request that an animal must be made available to him and that he should be allowed to slaughter it. Something which comes out from the heart definitely has its effect. Hence, they were affected and sold him a sheep which he very happily paid for. On the 10th of Dhul Hijjah, he offered the Qurbāni calling out the Takbeer in a loud voice in that remote land where the Sunnah of Ibrāheem عليه السلام had not been carried out since the fall of the Islamic rule. *(Hayaate Shaikhul Hind - Akābire Deoband aur ishqe Rasūl pg. 32)*

Lesson, One of the main reasons for us 'singing the praises' of our Akābir (senior 'Ulama) is the strict adherence to the Sunnah that was outstanding in their lives. The above incident is an example of one.

May Allāh ﷻ also inspire us to fulfil this great act and every other Sunnah of our Rasūlullāh ﷺ with the greatest passion and allow us to follow in the footsteps of these illustrious personalities, Āmeen.

The Status of Sayyidah Āishah

قَالَ بَعْضُ أَهْلِ التَّحْقِيْقِ إِنَّ يُوْسُفَ عَلَيْهِ السَّلَامُ لَمَّا رُمِيَ بِالْفَاحِشَةِ بَرَّأَهُ اللهُ عَلَى لِسَانِ صَبِيٍّ فِي الْمَهْدِ وَإِنَّ مَرْيَمَ لَمَّا رُمِيَتْ بِالْفَاحِشَةِ بَرَّأَهَا اللهُ عَلَى لِسَانِ ابْنِهَا عِيْسَى صَلَوَاتُ اللهِ عَلَيْهِ وَإِنَّ عَائِشَةَ لَمَّا رُمِيَتْ بِالْفَاحِشَةِ بَرَّأَهَا اللهُ تَعَالَى بِالْقُرْآنِ فَمَا رَضِيَ لَهَا بِبَرَاءَةِ صَبِيٍّ وَلَا نَبِيٍّ حَتَّى بَرَّأَهَا اللهُ بِكَلَامِهِ مِنَ الْقَذْفِ وَالْبُهْتَانِ

Some of the Islamic researchers have stated that when Prophet Yūsuf عليه السلام was accused of immorality, Allāh ﷻ announced his innocence on the tongue of a child in the cradle. When Maryam عليها السلام

12

was slandered, Allāh ﷻ declared her purity on the tongue of her
son, Eesā عليه السلام. However, when it came to the allegations against
Āishah رضي الله عنها, Allāh ﷻ clarified her innocence through the Glorious
Qur'ān. It was neither a Prophet nor a child; rather, it was the
Speech of Allāh ﷻ itself, that declared her innocence from the
smear and false allegation. *(Echoes From the Cave)*

12 Tips To Boost Your Salāh

It just doesn't feel the same . . . I lost it . . . How can I get it back?
Get ready for the ultimate Salāh-booster; a set of amazing productivity tips to enhance your prayer, give you a fresh perspective on
the world of Salāh, and make you love your prayer like never before, Inshā Allāh!

Allāh ﷻ advises, **"Seek help through patience and prayer, and indeed, it is difficult except for the humble ones."** (2:45)

Below are productivity tips based on a summary of a speech 'How
To Taste The True Beauty Of Salāh Series' by Mish'āri Al Kharrāz,

1. Say Allāhu Akbar and throw the world behind you.
Did you ever think, "Why do we start our prayer with Allāhu Akbar not with Subhān Allāh?" Realise that when you say Allāhu Akbar, you affirm that the One before Whom you are about to stand,
is greater than anything occupying you at that moment— greater
than your sleep, your families, your bills and your worries. Just imagine that when you say Allāhu Akbar while raising your hands,
you are throwing all of that behind you!

2. Visualise the veil.

When you stand to pray, Allāh 🕮 commands, Raise the veils from between Me and My servant! As soon as you say, 'Allāhu Akbar' and start your prayer, Allāh 🕮 sets His beautiful face to yours and does not turn away from you, unless you do. When your thoughts or your sight drifts off, He orders the veils to be drawn back down. Visualise these veils being lifted to keep concentration with your heart and body. Are you still drifting? This is why you repeat the great words, 'Allāhu Akbar' as you move into each position; it is a reminder and a new chance again and again to focus!

3. Salute the King.

Imagine walking into a palace; how would you recognise the servants of the king? Probably by their humble position of looking down. As you lower your gaze to the place of your prostration and place your hands right over left and close to your chest, it is time to salute the King. Imagine standing in front of Allāh 🕮 as you utter this beautiful salutation and feel each word, How perfect You are O Allāh and I praise You. Blessed be Your name, lofty is Your position and none has the right to be worshipped except You.
Realise that only the parts of Salāh you are mindful of are being accepted and that Shaytān does his very best to steal every sweet moment you have with Allāh 🕮!

4. Feel each verse of Sūrah Al-Fātihah is answered.

You are now ready to enter the essence of it all, Sūrah Al-Fātihah, the greatest Sūrah of the Qur'ān, without which your prayer is nullified. Know that Allāh 🕮 Himself answers back when you recite Sūrah Al-Fātihah, so add a short pause after each verse, feeling this

14

amazing dialogue. How can you ever drift off in this part of the prayer?

5. Utter His Name with pure love.
What has brought you to stand here right now? It is your love and longing to be with Allāh ﷻ. And when you meet up with your beloved, what do you first say? The sweet sound of the beloved's name, the name that blesses everything it falls upon! Feel Bismillāhir-Rahmānir-Raheem soothing your heart as it gently rolls off your lips.

6. Stand still at, "The Lord of the worlds."
The Prophet ﷺ told us, "Alhamdulillāh fills the scale!" (Muslim) Really feel the gratefulness when you say Alhamdulillāh. Did you see those documentaries where they zoom out from the cells of a plant's leaf all the way to the planets and galaxies? Now instead of that leaf, start the zoom out process with the image of yourself standing before Allāh ﷻ. Then zoom back down, back through the universe, to the place you are standing in prayer. The next time you pray view yourself from above and far away and truly taste the meaning of Rabbil Ālameen (Lord of the worlds)!

7. Reflect on Ar-Rahmānir Raheem before Māliki Yawmid-Deen.
Have you ever wondered why Allāh's ﷻ Names Ar-Rahmān and Ar-Raheem come before Māliki Yawmid-Deen (Master of the Day of Judgement)? Be reminded that it is the Most Gracious and Merciful who will judge us on the Day of Judgement! So feel empowered and comforted when you say Ar-Rahmānir-Raheem and then

pause a moment at Māliki Yawmid-Deen, realising the horrors of that Day.

8. Know what Iyyāka Na'budu wa Iyyāka Nasta'een really means.

You alone we worship and unto You alone we turn for help. Let this remind you to make Allāh 🕮 alone your focus, not the people. So when you are asked, why did you do this or that (deed), you can firmly answer, for Allāh 🕮! Feel this verse by knowing that the Salaf (predecessors) used to weep for hours reciting it. One of them was once praying in Makkah. His friend went ahead and did the Tawāf and when he returned to him, he was still at this verse, repeating it and crying until the sun came up.

9. Say Āmeen as if your life depended on it.

The most comprehensive supplication you can make is, Ihdinas-Sirātal-Mustaqeem (Guide us to the straight path). See how you followed the proper etiquettes of how to ask Allāh 🕮? You started glorifying and praising Him and then you make your request, Guide us. Now realise that your entire existence depends on this supplication. The Āmeen you will pronounce now will have to come from the bottom of your heart. Āmeen means, My Lord, grant or answer (my prayers). Say Āmeen as if you have been sentenced to death and are pleading for pardon, begging with passion.

10. Feel the bond with your Lord.

When you say Subhāna Rabbi-yal-'Adheem (How perfect is my Lord, the Supreme) in Ruku, focus on the pronoun that means my (in Rabbi). It adds that element of bonding, He is my Lord Who raised me in His care and who is nurturing me. Know the Prophet and the Companions ﷺ used to be in the bowing position nearly as long as they would be in the standing segment of Salāh. One Companion ﷺ said that he recited Al Fātihah, then Al Baqarah, Al-Imrān, An-Nisā' and Al-Mā'idah and the Companion, Abdullāh Ibn Zubair ﷺ was beside him, still in his Ruku!

11. Win the grand finale, your Sujood.

Your Sujood is the ultimate symbol of complete submission to your Creator. The Prophet ﷺ said, "The closest that a servant is to his Lord is when he is in prostration." (Muslim) "Prostrate much because there is no Muslim that prostrates to Allāh ﷻ except that Allāh ﷻ raises him one degree in Paradise by it and forgives for him a sin." (Ahmad) Imagine you are being raised one degree in Paradise with each Sujood and a sin falls off you with each prostration. Prostrate with body, heart and soul and taste the sweetest feeling in the world!

12. Supplicate before the Tasleem (Salām).

After the words of the Tashahhud (sitting position at the end of prayer) and before the Tasleem (saying Salām to indicate the end of prayer), there is a precious moment many waste! When the Prophet ﷺ taught Abdullāh Ibn Mas'ood ﷺ the Tashahhud, he said, "Then let him choose whatever supplication he wishes" (Bukhāri, Muslim). Just before you say Tasleem, make at least three heartfelt Du'ās to benefit from this treasure chest instead of rushing to say the Salām!

Remember this, the sweetness of this life lies in remembering Him, the sweetness of the next life lies in seeing Him! The next time you proceed for prayer, go because you love Him, go because you miss

Him and long to be with Him. Feel your heart flutter. Only then, will you be on your way to attaining that inner peace and comfort, which Salāh was prescribed for. *(Mishāri Al-Kharrāz)*

A Poem in Response to the Blasphemy of Our Beloved Prophet ﷺ

Has it ever crossed your mind whom they attack?
Aren't you mind-boggled by their blasphemous track?
They should rather mind with Tom, Harry and Jack.
Not with a Prophet revered by nations, white and black.

They wish to defame he who has the finest name.
Whose reputation has outlawed every attempt of blame.
Haven't they always been trying to cause him pain,
Yet, they were always buried in shame.

The Jewel of all the Prophets of the past till Judgement Day,
His law was revealed to last.
He taught man the Divine manner to pray and fast,
Like every Prophet, he was of the finest caste.
From the children of Ibrāheem عليه السلام, "the praiseworthy,
He would be called, 'The Truthful', 'The Trustworthy."
Eesa عليه السلام said, "He would be the most praiseworthy in appearance,
To Eesa عليه السلام his nation is more worthy."
He was the most handsome among one and all,

He out-shone anything on which moon light would fall.
Miraculously, he always appeared to be the most tall.
A lifetime he spent making the Divine call.

Simplicity was the highlight of his noble culture,
His guidance encompassed even trade and agriculture.
People embraced his call from a global multi-culture,
To the finest degree, their character would he then culture.

A villager once entered his holy mosque and in a corner began to urinate.
The Companions ﷺ were enraged at this uncultured trait,
His compassion surpassed them, so he told them to wait.
After the man was relieved, he only said, "This is where we prostrate."

A new Muslim, whilst praying, did not cease to speak.
People stared at him, till he almost gave a shriek.
Later the Prophet ﷺ carefully explained that in prayer we do not speak.
His remark, "I've never met a teacher with such wonderful technique."

A family was waylaid on some lonely road.
A boy was taken and as a slave was sold.
Some years later, he was as precious as gold,
He was gifted to Muhammad ﷺ, so he entered into his fold.

This slave's father learnt where he was.

He wished to release him with coins filled in jars.
But the boy said, "No, like my master there isn't any stars,
His character has reached far beyond Mars."
Another teenager served him from ten to twenty,
This age of adolescence has the most vulnerability.
Says the boy, "At times I would forget to carry out my duty,
But never was I ever made to feel guilty."

In the 90s, a man embraced the wonderful Islamic culture.
We enquired the reason for his excellent venture.
He read a book about the greatest preacher.
So we asked what was that attractive lustre.

He looked down to think about the magnetic feature.
Then he exclaimed, "Muhammad ﷺ was a unique creature,
his entire life was of an excellent nature.
He was the best and the noblest fixture."

To Madeenah he migrated to teach and foster.
A Rabbi came to witness the pearls of the greatest oyster.
He remarked, "This isn't the face of any imposter.
He is the Messiah, the final Prophet on the roster."
Embracing Islām, the Rabbi embarks upon a research,
To witness all the Prophetic signs, in a tireless search.
One day when questioned about him, he replied without a surge, '
"I can doubt my son's pedigree, in case my wife left me in the lurch.
"But the veracity of this Prophet, doubt cannot rupture,

His description which is in the Torah, the divine scripture.
That was conveyed by Jibreel ﷺ, the heavenly teacher
To the prophet Mūsa ﷺ, the trustworthy preacher."

In conclusion, everyone is invited to conduct a search,
And not succumb to what is posed as research.
For it is easy for man, from the truth, to diverge,
And find himself following some baseless 'research'.

(Mufti Ayub Jeena)

The Glass is Half-Full...!!!

From time to time, we all experience challenges. It could be when we encounter some difficult situations in our life or business, or we have problems with health, or even just day to day issues. What is really important is how we face up and react to those challenges. Our attitude and trust in our Creator will determine how much we succeed.

Attitude leads to altitude!

According to scientists, the bumble bee's body is too heavy and its wing span is too small. Aerodynamically, the bumble bee cannot fly. However, the bumble bee does not know that and it keeps flying.

When you do not know your limitations, you go out and surprise yourself. In hindsight, you wonder if you had any limitations! The only limitations a person has are those that are self-imposed. Do not let physical conditions dictate how you respond to life's challenges.

There is a story about a group of small frogs who took part in a race. The goal was to reach the top of a very high tower. A big crowd had gathered around the tower to see the race and cheer on the contestants. Then they were off!

No one in the crowd really believed that the tiny frogs would reach the top of the tower and they began to yell things like, "Oh, way too difficult!!", "They will never make it to the top" and "Not a chance that they will succeed. The tower is too high!"

The tiny frogs began collapsing one by one, but there were some that were managing to climb higher and higher.

The crowd continued to yell, "It is too difficult!!! No one will make it!"

More tiny frogs got tired and gave up. However, one frog continued higher and higher and higher. This one wasn't giving up!

At the end, every other frog had given up climbing the tower except for the one tiny frog who, after great effort, was the only one who reached the top! All of the other tiny frogs naturally wanted to know how this one frog managed to do it?

A contestant asked the tiny frog who had succeeded, how it had found the strength to reach the goal?

It turned out...that the winner was deaf.

Never listen to people who have a tendency of being negative or are pessimistic because they may impede your progress and stop you from achieving your dreams. Everything that you hear and see can affect you in so many ways. So filter and entertain only those that will have a positive bearing on your life.

"Indeed, Allāh will not change the condition of a nation until they change what is in themselves." (13:11)

So where do we start?..Changing our attitude to positive mode is vital! Therefore, always trust in Allāh ﷻ, be positive and think I can do this!

Remember, an optimist will see an opportunity in every difficulty whereas, a pessimist will see a difficulty in every opportunity.

Is the glass half full or half empty? Your attitude will decide!

By Abū Muhammad Yūsuf

Comments of People

Shaykh Muhammad Zakariyyah ﷺ once mentioned,

My beloved friends! As long as you are treading upon the Sunnah, do not be concerned and worried about what people have to say; whether they have a low opinion of you or regard you to be insane. The Prophets ﷺ were not spared by the people and similarly, our pious predecessors were also labelled with many names. Hence, if you become a target of people's criticism (due to treading on Deen), then why do you let this worry you? Keep your pious predecessors before you as your example - those pious predecessors who remained devoted and committed to the Sunnah of Rasūlullāh ﷺ under all circumstances. *(Malfoozāte Hadhrat Shaykh 1/136)*

Upbringing of Children

I generally, am quite an optimistic person. I tend to believe that everything will work out for the best unless the evidence is over-whelmingly to the contrary and anyone who knows me, will tell you that I am not prone to drama. That's why when I say that modern parenting is in serious trouble - crisis, even - I hope you will listen and listen carefully. I have worked with children and their parents across two continents and two decades and what I have seen in recent years alarms me. Here are the greatest problems, as I see them,

1. **A fear of our children**. I have what I think of as "The Sippy Cup Test," wherein, I will observe a parent getting her toddler a cup of milk in the morning. If the child says, "I want the pink Sippy cup, not the blue!" yet the mum has already poured the milk into the blue Sippy cup, I watch carefully to see how the parent reacts. More often than not, the mum's face whitens and she rushes to get the preferred Sippy cup before the child has a tantrum. Fail! What are you afraid of, mum? Who is in charge here? Let her have a tantrum and remove yourself so you don't have to hear it. But for goodness' sake, do not make extra work for yourself just to please her - and even more importantly, think about the lesson it teaches if you give her what she wants because she has thrown a fit.

2. **A lowered bar**. When children misbehave, whether it is by way of public outburst or private surliness, parents are apt to shrug their shoulders as if to say, "That's just the way it is with

kids." I assure you, it doesn't have to be. Children are capable of much more than what parents typically expect from them, whether it is in the form of proper manners, respect for elders, chores, generosity or self-control. You do not think a child can sit through dinner at a restaurant? Rubbish. You do not think a child can clear the table without being asked? Rubbish again! The only reason they do not behave is because you have not shown them how and you have not expected it! It is that simple. Raise the bar and your child shall rise to the occasion.

3. **We have lost the village.** It used to be that bus drivers, teachers, shopkeepers and other parents had carte blanche to correct an unruly child. They would act as the mum and dad's eyes and ears when their children were out of sight and everyone worked towards the same shared interest, raising proper boys and girls. This village was one of support. Now, when someone who is not the child's parent dares to correct him, the mum and dad get upset. They want their child to appear perfect and so they often do not accept teachers' and others' reports that he is not. They will storm in and have a go at a teacher rather than discipline their child for acting out in class. They feel the need to project a perfect picture to the world and unfortunately, their insecurity is reinforced because many parents do judge one another. If a child is having a tantrum, all eyes turn on the mum disapprovingly. Instead she should be supported because chances are, the tantrum occurred because she is not giving in to one of her child's demands. Those observers should instead be saying, "Hey, good work - I know setting limits is hard."

4. **A reliance on shortcuts.** I think it is wonderful that parents have all sorts of electronics to help them through airline flights and long waits at the doctor's office. It is equally fabulous that we can order our groceries online for delivery and heat up healthy-ish food at the touch of a button on the microwave. Parents are busier than ever and I am all for taking the easy way when you need it. But shortcuts can be a slippery slope. When you see how wonderful it is that Caillou can entertain your child on a flight, do not be tempted to put it on when you are at a restaurant. Children must still learn patience. They must still learn to entertain themselves. They must still learn that not all food comes out steaming hot and ready in three minutes or less and ideally, they will also learn to help prepare it. Babies must learn to self-soothe instead of sitting in a vibrating chair each time they are fussy. Toddlers need to pick themselves up when they fall down instead of just raising their arms to mum and dad. Show children that shortcuts can be helpful, but that there is great satisfaction in doing things the slow way too.

5. **Parents put their children's needs ahead of their own.** Naturally, parents are wired to take care of their children first and this is a good thing for evolution! I am an advocate of adhering to a schedule that suits your child's needs and of practices like feeding and clothing your children first. But parents today have taken it too far, completely subsuming their own needs and mental health for the sake of their children. So often I see mums get up from bed again and again, to fulfil the whims of their child. Or dads drop everything to run across the zoo to get their daughter a drink because she is thirsty. There is nothing wrong with not going to your child

when she wants yet another glass of water at night. There is nothing wrong with that dad at the zoo saying, "Absolutely, you can have something to drink, but you must wait until we pass the next drinking fountain." There is nothing wrong with using the word "No" on occasion. There is nothing wrong with asking your child to entertain herself for a few minutes because mummy would like to use the toilet in private or flick through a magazine for that matter.

I fear that if we do not start to correct these five grave parenting mistakes, and soon, the children we are raising will grow up to be entitled, selfish, impatient and rude adults. It will not be their fault - it will be ours. We never taught them any differently, we never expected any more of them. We never wanted them to feel any discomfort and so, when they inevitably do, they are woefully unprepared for it. So please, parents and caregivers, from London to Los Angeles and all over the world, ask more. Expect more. Share your struggles. Give less. And let us straighten these children out together and prepare them for what they need to be successful in the real world and not the sheltered one we have made for them.

Advice For Teachers

Shaykh Shamsul Haq Afghāni ﷺ used to say (addressing the teachers);
"The teacher should peruse (research a subject) three times;
The first time for (his personal) understanding (of that subject), the second time to make others understand and the third time to facilitate its understanding (for others)."

Taqleed

Taqleed-Linguistically and Islamically.

Taqleed is from the root word قلادة (Qaladah)meaning, something placed around a neck. It is used to describe something around the neck of an animal to keep it under control, like a rope or a collar as well as anything around the neck of a human, like a necklace in which case it is used to beautify a person.

The word قلادة (Qaladah) is used in the Qur'ān to describe the rope around the neck of an animal but Sayyidah Āishah ﷺ also used this word as a necklace when narrating the incident which lead to the hypocrites slandering her. In Arabic, many nouns, verbs and adjectives have a common root which is varied to give a suitable meaning. The word - علم (Ilm) means knowledge and the effort of acquiring knowledge is تعليم (Ta'leem).

30

Similarly, linguistically the literal meaning of Taqleed is, "To obey and follow anyone" and Islamically, it has come to imply, "To accept as Hujjat (evidence) and authority the rulings and verdicts of anyone not specified in Shariah, without the demand of evidence." This does not mean that there is not evidence for what they have ruled e.g. the Taqleed of the four Mujtahid Imāms. The Taqleed of any one of them is not specified in Qur'ān or Hadeeth but to accept their rulings and verdicts without demanding evidence is referred to as Taqleed and those who accept their rulings are referred to as "Muqallids".

Many things by nature are neither good nor bad but their use will determine if they are good or bad. For example, friendship; a good friend is undoubtedly good but a bad friend is undoubtedly bad. Meat of a Halāl animal slaughtered in the proper way is Halāl but that of a Harām animal or a Halāl animal but slaughtered wrongly, would be Harām.

Likewise, Taqleed of bad people, especially disbelievers, who do not believe, obey nor worship Allāh ﷻ is undoubtedly bad and such Taqleed is definitely detrimental to ones Deen and faith. However, the Taqleed of those whom the Ummah has acknowledged to be amongst the most learned, most pious and most sincere from the very early times of this Ummah can only be good and how possibly can that be otherwise?

Just as for an animal, who has a قلادة (Qalādah) around it's neck and is on a lead, nobody will dare to hurt or harm it as they can see that it is being lead by it's master. However, an animal without a lead, could easily be put down by law enforcement authorities.

So for a Muslim who wears a قلادة (Qalādah) the necklace of Taqleed of the pious, highly knowledgeable Mujtahids, can only be a guarantee of safety of his Deen.

George and Eid-ul-Adhā

George is an American who is over 50 years old. He lives in Washington with his wife, his son and his daughter.

When Dhul Hijjah was coming near, George and his family started to follow the news closely to know when Dhul Hijjah will start exactly. He watched the TV, his wife listened to the radio and his son surfed Islamic sites on the internet … everyone eagerly waiting for any news.

When they discovered the start of Dhul Hijjah, they prepared themselves for Eid ul-Adha, which is on the 10th of Dhul Hijjah, following the Day of Arafah on the 9th.

The next day, the family drove to the countryside to buy a sheep. They chose the sheep carefully, in accordance with the Islamic guidelines, in order to slaughter it on the first day of Eid. They carried the sheep with them in the car and on their way back, the little girl was expressing her joy for the coming Eid. She told her father, "Oh dad how I love Eid! I'll get to wear my new dress, play with my new doll, and go out with my friends to the park. Oh how I wish all the days of the year were Eid!"

When they got home, the wife told her husband George, "I've read that it is prescribed to divide our sacrifice into three parts, a third we give to the poor and the needy, a third we gift to our neighbours, Elizabeth, David and Mark and a third we eat from and save for the coming weeks."

When the day of Eid came, they were confused where the exact direction of the Qiblah was. They assumed that it was in a certain direction towards Makkah and that this should be sufficient. George held the knife, placed the sheep towards the Qiblah and slaughtered it. The wife then divided the meat into three parts as they agreed. Suddenly, George remembered something and shouted to his family, "We're late for church! Today is Sunday, and we'll miss the Sunday Mass!" George never missed church on Sunday. Rather, he always made sure to take his wife and children with him.

At that point, the speaker had finished his story about George and his family. One person from the audience exclaimed, "You confused us with this story of yours!! Is George a Muslim or a Christian?!"

The speaker, Ahmad, replied, "George and his family are Christians. They do not believe that Allāh ﷻ is One, rather, they believe He is the third of three. They also do not believe that Prophet Muhammad ﷺ is the last and final Messenger."

Chattering and mumbling erupted among the audience, and then a voice from the crowd said, "Do not lie to us Ahmad! Who would believe that George and his family would do all that and be Christian?! Why would a Christian perform all these rituals of Islām and Muslims? From following the news closely in order to determine the start of Dhul Hijjah and the specific day of Eid, to buying a sheep from his own money and slaughtering it as is prescribed in Islām, etc."

Ahmad said with a smile on his face, "My beloved brothers, why do you find it so hard to believe my story? Why can't you believe that such a Christian family exist? Isn't there in our Muslim countries an Abdullāh, a Muhammad, a Khālid, a Khadeejah and a Fātimah, who celebrate Christian or Jewish Festivals? Don't we see Muslims celebrating New Years, Christmas, Valentines, Halloween, Easter, Birthdays etc.? Why is this story so surprising then? Why is it that we do not see Jews celebrating our Festivals or the Festivals of the Christians? Is it not because each one has his own Religion and Beliefs and has his own Festivals? Why were we so surprised of George being a Christian who celebrates our Eid, and are refusing his actions, while at the same time we are not surprised of our own actions?!"

Finally, Ahmad said, "I've lived in the U.S.A for more than ten years. I swear by Allāh, I never saw a Christian or a Jew celebrating any of our Eids. Neither have I heard any of them asking about our festivals and celebrations. Even when I invited them for Eidul-Fitr in my apartment, no one attended when they knew it was a religious festival. That is what I experienced during my stay in the West, but when I returned back to my Muslim country, I found Muslims celebrating their holidays. What shall I say except there is no power and no might except from Allāh ﷻ."

Path to Paradise

A lovely story with an Islamic theme - it won't leave your eyes dry!
I promise. Inshā Allāh.

Every Friday afternoon, after the Jumu'ah prayers, the Imām and
his eleven year old son would go out into their town and hand out
"Path to Paradise" and other Islamic literature. This particular and
fortunate friday afternoon, as the time came for the Imām and his
son to go to the streets with their booklets, it was very cold outside, as well as pouring rain. The boy bundled up in his warmest
and driest clothes and said, "OK, dad, I'm ready!" His dad asked,
"Ready for what?" "Dad, it is time we go out and distribute these
Islamic books."

Dad responds, "Son, it is very cold outside and it is pouring with
rain." The boy gives his dad a surprised look, asking, "But dad, are
not people still going to Hell, even though it is raining?" Dad answers, "Son, I am not going out in this weather.' Despondently, the
boy asks, 'Dad, can I go please?" His father hesitated for a moment
then said, 'Son, you can go. Here are the booklets. Be careful, okay
son." Thanks, dad!' And with that, he was off and out into the rain.

This eleven year old boy walked the streets of the town going door
to door and handing everybody he met in the street a pamphlet or
a booklet.

After two hours of walking in the rain, he was soaking, bone-chilled wet and down to his very last booklet. He stopped on a corner and looked for someone to hand a booklet to, but the streets were now totally deserted. Then he turned toward the first home he saw and started up the sidewalk to the front door and rang the door bell. He rang the bell, but nobody answered. He rang it again and again, but still no one answered. He waited but still no answer.

Finally, he turned to leave but something stopped him. Again, he turned to the door, rang the bell and knocked loudly on the door with his fist. He waited, something holding him there on the front porch. He rang again and this time the door slowly opened.

Standing in the doorway was a very sad-looking elderly lady. She softly asked, 'What can I do for you, son?'' With radiant eyes and a smile that lit up her world, this little boy said, "Ma'am, I'm sorry if I disturbed you, but I just want to tell you that Allāh ﷻ really loves you and cares for you and I came to give you my very last booklet which will tell you all about God, the real purpose of creation and how to achieve His pleasure." With that, he handed her his last booklet and turned to leave. She called to him as he departed. 'Thank you, son! And God Bless You!'

The following week on Friday afternoon after Jumu'ah prayers, the Imām was giving some lectures. As he always did in this western city, he concluded the lecture and asked,

'Does anybody have questions or want to say anything?'

Slowly, in the back row among the ladies, an elderly lady's voice was heard over the speaker. No one in this gathering knew her. She started to speak…"I've never been here before. You see, before last Friday I was not a Muslim, and never thought I could ever be. My husband died a few years ago, leaving me totally alone in this world. Last Friday, being a particularly cold and rainy day, I was contemplating, suicide as I had no hope left. So I took a rope and a chair and ascended the stairway into the attic of my home. I fastened the rope securely to a rafter in the roof, then stood on the chair and fastened the other end of the rope around my neck. Standing on that chair, so lonely and broken-hearted I was about to leap off when suddenly, the loud ringing of my doorbell downstairs startled me.

I thought, I'll wait a minute, and whoever it is will go away. I waited and waited, but the ringing doorbell seemed to get louder and more insistent and then, the person ringing also started knocking loudly..I thought to myself again, 'Who on earth could this be? Nobody ever rings my bell or comes to see me.'

I loosened the rope from my neck and started for the front door, all the while, the bell rang louder and louder. When I opened the door and looked I could hardly believe my eyes, for there on my front porch was the most radiant and angelic little boy I had ever seen in my life. His smile, oh, I could never describe it to you! The words that came from his mouth caused my heart that had long been dead to leap to life as he exclaimed with a cherub-like voice,

'Ma'am, I just came to tell you that Allāh ﷻ really loves and cares for you!'

'Then he gave me this booklet, 'Path To Paradise' that I now hold in my hand. As the little angel disappeared back out into the cold and rain, I closed my door and read slowly every word of this book. Then I went up to my attic to get my rope and chair. I wouldn't be needing them any more.

You see? I am now a Happy Vicegerent of the One True Allāh ﷻ. Since the address of your congregation was stamped on the back of this booklet, I have come here to personally say thank you to Allāh's ﷻ little angel who came just in the nick of time and by so doing, spared my soul from an eternity in Hell."

There was not a dry eye in the Masjid. The shouts of Takbeer..Allāhu Akbar. rented the air.

The Imām descended from the pulpit to the front row where the little angel was seated. He took his son in his arms and sobbed uncontrollably. Probably, no Jamā'at has had a more glorious moment and probably, this universe has never seen a father that was more filled with love and honour for his son.. Except for one. this very one..

Remember, Allāh's ﷻ message can make the difference in your life!

Sayyidunā Julaybeeb ﷺ

It is narrated in the books of history that Julaybeeb ﷺ was a Sahābi who was short in height and deformed in appearance. His lineage was not known, no one knew who his parents were, he had no clan to protect him and no tribe willing to accept him as their own. He was a lonely figure. Even the small children of Madeenah would tease and mock him. Owing to his disabilities no one would allow him to sit in their company.

He survived as best as he could. Many a lonely night in Madeenah he spent wondering the streets in despair. Tears of desperation would run down his cheeks. There was no one willing to offer him love or compassion. He had no family and not a single friend in the world. Life for him was a lonely struggle.

After the arrival of the Prophet of Allāh ﷺ to Madeenah, the fortunes of Julaybeeb ﷺ changed. He would go and sit in the company of the Prophet ﷺ and listen intently, rarely speaking. He out of shyness would keep his gaze lowered. He now had the best of friends in the Prophet of Allāh ﷺ. Those days of loneliness and despair were over for the best of creation had arrived. Julaybeeb ﷺ was now part of the community of believers.

One day, as he was sitting in the company of the Prophet ﷺ, the Messenger of Allāh ﷺ asked him, "O Julaybeeb ﷺ, ask for something; is there anything you desire?"

He raised his head slowly and said in a shy voice,
"O Messenger of Allāh ﷺ, Allāh ﷻ has blessed me with your
companionship. I get to sit at your blessed feet and hear your
blessed words, what more could I desire?"

The Prophet of Allāh ﷺ asked, "How would you like to get
married, my dear Julaybeeb?" He smiled shyly, wondering who
would want to marry him. "Yes Messenger of Allāh ﷺ, I would like
that."

The Prophet of Allāh ﷺ went to the house of a prominent and
noble Sahābi from amongst the Ansār. He said, "I have come to ask
for your daughter's hand in marriage." The Sahābi was overjoyed,
he said, "O Messenger of Allāh ﷺ what could be a greater blessing
than this?"

The Prophet ﷺ said, "I do not ask of her for myself, it is for
Julaybeeb that I am asking. "The Sahābi was left stunned, "For
Julaybeeb?" he asked in bewilderment. "Yes for Julaybeeb", replied the Messenger of Allāh ﷺ. He said, "Let me consult with my
wife."

He went and told her. "The Prophet of Allāh ﷺ has asked for your
daughter's hand in marriage for Julaybeeb." She started crying and
wailing "No, not Julaybeeb; anyone but Jualybeeb! I will never allow this!"

Upon hearing the commotion, the daughter arrived. It is said that
she was so beautiful that there was none among the women of the

Ansār who could compete with her looks. She was so shy and modest that perhaps the sky itself had never seen her head uncovered. She had so much Taqwa that she would spend her days and nights in worship.

The daughter asked what was happening. She was told that the Prophet of Allāh ﷺ wanted her hand in marriage for Julaybeeb ﷺ. As the mother continued her crying and wailing, the daughter spoke and said, " O my mother, fear Allāh ﷻ; think of what you are saying. Are you turning away the Prophet of Allāh ﷺ? 'O' my mother, it does not suit a believer to make their own decision once Allāh ﷻ and His Messenger ﷺ have decided on a matter. Do you think that the Prophet of Allāh ﷺ will disgrace us? How blessed is the status of Julaybeeb ﷺ, that Allāh ﷻ and His Messenger ﷺ are asking for your daughter's hand on his behalf? Don't you know that the angels themselves envy the dust on the feet of one who is a beloved of Allāh ﷻ and His Prophet ﷺ? Ask the Prophet ﷺ to send me Julaybeeb ﷺ for there is no greater privilege than for me to be blessed by such a husband. The Prophet of Allāh ﷺ has arrived with such a wonderful gift, yet my mother, you cry and wail."

The mother's heart being filled with remorse said, "Stop my daughter, do not say another word. Indeed I have erred, I repent and I repent a thousand times over, for as of this moment there is no one who I would prefer for you more than Julaybeeb."

The following day the Nikāh was conducted. Sayyidunā Uthmān ﷺ and Sayyidunā Ali ﷺ presented Julaybeeb ﷺ with a gift of money to help arrange the feast of Waleemah and to purchase accommodation.

A short time later on an expedition, Julaybeeb ﷺ was martyred.
On the day of the expedition, his father in-law had pleaded with
him, "'O' Julaybeeb, this is just an expedition. It is not a compulso-
ry, it is Fardh Kifāyah, it is voluntary. You are newly married, so
spend some time with your wife."

Julaybeeb ﷺ, the one who had spent a lifetime in despair, had now
found a loving wife. However, listen to his response to the father
in-law's request. He said, "O my father, you say a strange thing.
My beloved Prophet ﷺ is in the battlefield facing the enemies and
you want me to sit at home with my wife? Nay, I will sacrifice my
blood and my soul rather than see my Prophet ﷺ facing hardship
while I sit at home in luxury."

The diminutive Julaybeeb ﷺ was indeed a strange sight carrying a
sword almost the same size as him. The Sahābah ﷺ stared in won-
derment at him; the sweet and gentle Julaybeeb ﷺ was transformed into a lion. "Who dare wage war upon my Prophet ﷺ?" he
said, as he charged into the ranks of the enemy.

After the battle, the Prophet of Allāh ﷺ asked the Sahābah ﷺ to go
and see if anyone was missing from their families and clans. Each
one returned accounting for all his family members. Then the
Prophet ﷺ spoke with tears in his eyes and said, "But I have lost
my beloved Julaybeeb. Go and find him." They found his diminutive body lying next to seven disbelievers he had slain in the battle.

The Prophet of Allāh ﷺ asked for a grave to be dug. As he held the
body of Julaybeeb ﷺ, he said, "O' Allāh ﷺ, he is from me and I am

from him." He repeated this three times. The Companions wept profusely, "May our mothers and fathers be sacrificed for you O' Julaybeeb, how great is your status." Thus, a Sahābi ﷺ who had once lived as an outcast, shunned by the society around him, loved Allāh ﷻ and His Messenger ﷺ and reached such a high status. He who was not good looking was blessed with a beautiful wife. He who was poor, was blessed by a wealthy wife. He who had no family or status, was blessed by a wife with noble status and lineage. He had lived in loneliness and despair but was loved by Allāh ﷻ and His Messenger ﷺ. He had the Messenger of Allāh ﷺ say, " O Allāh ﷻ, he is from me and I am from him."

It is said that upon his martyrdom, the sky itself was filled with thousands of angels who had come to participate in his Janāzah!

Julaybeeb ﷺ 'The Lonesome One' had become a beloved of Allāh ﷻ and his Prophet ﷺ. He was lonely no more. Such is the status of the lovers of the Prophet ﷺ.

As for his wife, it is said that there was no widow whose hand was more sought after in marriage than hers.

Two Types of Love

During the blessed journey to Makkah and Madeenah, Shaykh
Zulfiqār Sāhib said, The fatherly love is somewhat different to the
motherly love. A father loves the child but at the same time he has
to show some Jalāl (awe) as well. This is necessary for the Tarbiyah
(upbringing) of the child. The mother's love is more to do with
affection and feelings for the child. She knows her child more than
anyone else. She wants everything best for her child.

This is the case with these two cities (Makkah and Madeenah). In
Makkah Mukarramah, there is Jalāl of Allāh ﷻ. The Greatness and
the Majesty of Allāh ﷻ is portrayed here. The pilgrims love Allāh
ﷻ and He loves the pilgrims. However, there is Tawāf, loud cries
of Du'ās and pushing and shoving. This portrays the Majesty of
Allāh ﷻ; His Majesty is affecting those doing tawāf. He is blessing
them in a special way.

In Madeenah Munawwarah, there is Jamāl (calmness). The calmness, serenity and peaceful environment of Madeenah Munawwarah is amazing. Rasūlullāh ﷺ is there. He is eager for us to have the
best of everything. He loves his followers, so he focuses his attention towards them. It is up to us now that while we are there, we
pay his Rawdhah (grave) a regular visit and stay close to his
Rawdhah. Go for Salām from the front at least once everyday.
Whilst sitting in the Masjid, go in Murāqabah (meditation), close
your eyes and feel the Fuyooz (blessings) of Rasūlullāh ﷺ coming
into your hearts like the water that flows from a large river to various streams.

Shaykh Zulfiqār Sāhib went on to mention the love of the Sahābah ⬥ for Rasūlullāh ⬥. He said Rasūlullāh ⬥ was 'Mahboobe Kul Jahān' i.e. the whole universe loved him. He gave examples of Jamādāt (non living objects) , Nabātāt (plants) , Haywānāt's (animals) love for him. Then he gave examples of how the Companions loved him.

He also said we have to undertake this journey with great love and keep reciting Durood Shareef along the way or recite Qur'ān Shareef.

Imām Shāfi'ee ⬥ went from Makkah Mukarramah to Madeenah Munawwarah. It took him 16 days to get there. He says, I used to complete the entire Qur'ān recitation everyday. Thus, I did 16 Khatams (completion) before reaching there."

Shaykh said, "Whatever you recite, give that as a gift to Rasūlullāh ⬥. When a person goes to meet someone senior, he takes a gift for them. This will be your gift for him."

10 Days of Dhul Hijjah

"There are no days in which righteous deeds are more beloved to Allah ⬥ than these 10 days." [Bukhāri]

"There are no days greater in the sight of Allāh ⬥ (including Ramadhān) and in which righteous deeds are more beloved to Him than these 10 days, so during this time recite a great deal of

Tahleel ("Lā ilāha illallāh"), Takbeer (Allāhu Akbar) and Tahmeed (Alhamdu Lillāh)." [Ahmad]

A Sunnah of the Prophet ﷺ,
"When you see the new moon of Dhul-Hijjah, if any one of you wants to offer a sacrifice, then he should stop cutting his hair and nails until he has offered his sacrifice." [Muslim]

Another Sunnah,
"The Prophet ﷺ used to fast on the first 9 days of Dhul-Hijjah and the day of 'Āshoora' and 3 days each month". [Nasa'i, Abū Dāwood]

Fasting on the Day of Arafah,
The Holy Prophet ﷺ said, "It expiates for the sins of the previous year and of the coming year." [Muslim]

"There is no day on which Allāh ﷻ frees more people from the fire than the Day of Arafah. He comes close and expresses His pride to the angels, saying, "What do these people want?" [Muslim]

Takbeer of Tashreeq,
After each Fardh Salāh recite from the Fajr of 9th Dhul Hijjah until the Asr of the 13th "Allāhu Akbar, Allāhu Akbar, Lā ilāha illallāhu, Wallāhu Akbar Allāhu Akbar, Wa Lil-lāhil-hamd (Allāh is the Greatest, Allāh is the Greatest, there is no god but Allāh; Allāh is the Greatest and to Allāh be all praise)."
Adjust your daily routines and make the most of these precious days.

47

Characteristics of a Pious Husband

On the Day of Judgement, Allāh ﷻ will ask men if they fulfilled their obligations towards their families. Those who fear Allāh ﷻ will do their best to direct the way their wives and children live by educating themselves and their families to living according to the Sunnah of the Prophet ﷺ and the Holy Qur'ān, the final word of Allāh ﷻ.

The following are advices for the husband from the Holy Qur'ān and Sunnah.

1.   The Prophet ﷺ said, "The best of you is the best one to his family." [Tabarāni]
2.   "To share food with her, to provide her with (decent) clothes as he provides himself, to refrain from smacking her and not ignoring her." [Ahmad]
3.   "One should not hate his wife. If he dislikes some of her habits, he would (surely) like others (habits)." [Muslim]
4.   "A woman was created from a bent rib and will not be made straight for you on one way (that you like). If you want to enjoy her, you enjoy her while she is still bent. If you want to straighten her up, you will break her. Breaking her is divorcing her." [Bukhāri, Muslim]
5.   "Fast some days and do not fast in other days; pray at night (some portions) and sleep (in other portions). Your body has a right over you (to rest), your eye has a right over you (to sleep) and your wife has a right over you." [Bukhāri, Muslim]

6. "Fear Allāh ﷻ in treating women." [Muslim]
7. "Be advised to treat women righteously." [Bukhāri, Muslim]
8. **"And live with them honourably. If you dislike them, it may be that you dislike a thing that Allāh brings through it a great deal of good." [4,19]**
9. The Prophet ﷺ said, "(There is) a Dinār (a currency of the time) that you spend on your family, a Dinār that you spend on a poor person and a Dinār that you spend in the path of Allāh ﷻ. The one that carries the most reward is the one that you spend on your family." [Muslim]
10. The Prophet ﷺ said to Sa'd Ibn Abi Waqqās ؓ,"Know that there is no charity that you give, whether small or large, for the sake of Allāh ﷻ, but you will be rewarded for it, even the morsel (of food) that you put into your wife's mouth."

[Bukhāri, Muslim]

Natural Healers

Valuable Prescriptions;

Sayyidunā Abū Dardā ؓ narrates that a person who recites 7 times after Fajr and after Maghrib, the last part of the last verse of Sūrah Tawbah, in the eleventh Juz, Allāh ﷻ will suffice (protect) him from all the worries of the Dunya and Ākhirah. (Rūhul Maʿāni)

حَسْبِيَ اللهُ لَا إِلٰهَ إِلَّا هُوَ عَلَيْهِ تَوَكَّلْتُ وَهُوَ رَبُّ الْعَرْشِ الْعَظِيْمِ

"Allāh is sufficient for me; there is no deity but He; upon Him I rely and He is the Lord of the Great Throne." (9:129)

No matter what worry, anxiety, depression or pressure may be upon a person, and of whatever magnitude, Allāh ﷻ will protect him from it.

Shaykh Hakeem Muhammad Akhtar Sāhib ؒ would say that when the Swiss can manufacture a watch that is waterproof, such that even under 200 meters of water, the vapour does not enter it, what is the difficulty for Allāh ﷻ to make a heart that is 'worry-proof', even though the person is surrounded by worries?

Allāh's ﷻ protection extends to such heights that even the vapour of worry will not enter it.

(Taken from seven valuable prescriptions by Shaykh Abdul Hameed Ishāq Sāhib.)

An Exemplary Youth

This Ramadhān, Cii Radio's Mufti AK Hoosen embarked on a multi-country tour of South America, inspecting the Islamic infrastructure in various regions and offering encouragement to numerous South African Ulama who have settled in the region.

Ruminating on a touching encounter he had in Venezuela, Mufti AK Hoosen shared the following inspirational story about Hāzim, a young Palestinian immigrant whose sincere efforts for Deen have significantly transformed the Islamic landscape of the continent.

Hāzim was a young Palestinian brother whose family settled in South America decades ago. The family was very affluent but also far estranged from the practices of Islām. Allāh ﷻ endowed them with wealth you cannot dream of. They literally own an entire fleet of private jets and aeroplanes.

Subhān-Allāh, a South African Jamā'at visits the region, invites the Muslims of the area to Allāh ﷻ and the entire life trajectory of this family changes.

This young boy, Hāzim, develops a soft spot for the visitors and begins to serve them enthusiastically. It becomes clear that Allāh ﷻ has destined that he becomes a means of Hidāyah (guidance) for thousands of people.

He associates himself with the ideals championed by the Tableegh Jamā'at and almost immediately, draws flak from his own blood.

51

They oppose his affiliation to the Jamā'at totally. Matters deteriorate so badly that Hāzim is disowned.

Yet, the young man remains steadfast as a rock. He fends for himself and matures. He sells the only car that is still registered on his name to raise capital for a journey he is yearning to undertake. He heads off to the Indian subcontinent to immerse himself in the work and learn the principles of Tableegh.

On his return to Venezuela, fountains of Divine blessings begins to shower upon him. He is selected to represent his country at the international Qur'ān memorization competition in Makkah, even though he was not a Hāfidh. He is judged to be the most knowledgeable youngster in Qur'ān in the entire nation. In Makkah, Allāh ﷻ honours him with an opportunity to enter the Ka'bah even though he is barely 20.

All the while, Hāzim's relationship with his family remains rocky.

Hāzim gets married. Soon, his wife gives birth to a baby girl, Maryam.

Hāzim is recognised across Venezuela as the livewire of the effort of Tableegh. His stature is magnified because of his association with an influential and affluent immigrant family.

Then, one day, Hāzim inexplicably prepares a copy of his will. There is a Nikāh in the family, which his wife requests to attend. He agrees to take her there after he performs Ishā.

On his way to the Masjid, the Jāmiah Masjid in Valencia, as Allāh ﷻ decrees, Hāzim meets up in an accident. Just 26 years old and his soul is reunited with his Rabb (Lord).

There is a secret, as yet unrevealed. His wife is pregnant, but she intended to disclose the good news to him en route to the wedding after Ishā.

For one half of his life, he was Ma'soom (sinless) and from the age of 13, he was in the path of Allāh ﷻ, propagating and teaching the Deen. Hāzim is honoured further with the death of a martyr. Thousands of people flock to his funeral and send condolences from all parts of South America. Many attest to having learnt so much about the Deen from this young warrior.

His parents and siblings are ashamed, We opposed our son, but just look how bitterly people are mourning his departure. Look how much honour he has managed to garner.

The family experiences a re-awakening. They now follow in Hāzim's footsteps and also align themselves enthusiastically with the work of Tableegh. Their entire fleet of private jets and coffers of wealth are put to the service of the Deen.

One youngster makes so much sacrifice that today, South America – Brazil, Argentina, Venezuela and other countries – is dotted with Madāris and Islamic Institutes bearing Hāzim's name.

During my visit, I went to the graveyard were Hāzim was buried and made special Du'ā for this distinguished Dā'ee. All the graves surrounding his sported huge tombstones and memorials, but his was totally unmarked. So simple. You could feel that this man was specially accepted by Allāh 🕮.

Hāzim's wife gave birth and young Muhammad and Maryam together with their mother, today, continue holding aloft the torch of lofty ideals set into blaze by their beloved father.

You could imagine; it must have never been easy for a young man with no feet to stand on, to confront the pressure of his entire extended family. It would have been immensely difficult. However, Hāzim was sincere. He had Istiqāmah (steadfastness) and hence became Maqbool (accepted) by Allah 🕮.

We make Du'ā Allāh 🕮 also makes us Khādims (Servants of His Deen). Āmeen

A Strange Method of Du'ā

Imām Asma'i 🕮 says, I saw a bedouin standing in front of the grave of Rasūlullāh 🕮, saying the following words,

O' Allāh 🕮, this is Your beloved 🕮 and Shaytān is Your enemy and I am Your servant. If You forgive me, Your beloved 🕮 will become happy and Your enemy will be saddened and Your servant will be successful. And if You do not forgive me, Your beloved 🕮 will be saddened and Your enemy will be happy and Your servant will be destroyed. And You are more generous than to please Your enemy and to sadden Your beloved 🕮 and to destroy Your servant.

O' Allāh 🕮, verily the noblemen and the most generous of the Arabs would free a slave when standing in front of the graves of any of their great leaders and I am standing in front of the grave of the leader of the entire humanity, so O' Rabbul Ālameen (Lord of the worlds), free my soul from the fire of Hell."

Imām Asma'i 🕮 says, "I was amazed by his eloquence and strong case."

Qāri Ismāeel Sāhib 🌸

Shaykh Abdur Raheem Sāhib said, 'Our Ustād of Tajweed, Qāri Ismāeel Samni Sāhib 🌸 passed away this morning. He was diagnosed with stomach cancer and lived with it for the last few months. May Allāh 🌸 forgive him, shower His Rahmah (mercy) upon him and elevate his ranks. Āmeen.

We studied Qirāt with him. I also had the privilege of listening to his whole Qur'ān on two occasions. Once, in Ramadhān 1985, in Saharanpūr, UP India and once in Tahajjud during Ramadhān 1989, in Dārul Uloom Bury, during I'tikāf.

In 1985, I spent the whole month of Ramadhān in Saharanpūr with Hadhrat Maulāna Talha Sāhib in Dār Jadeed (new building). Qāri Sāhib 🌸 was also present in Saharanpūr. He would recite his Juz to me everyday after Asr. He was a jolly and talkative person. He would sometimes pause, narrate some stories, say a few words and then continue.

Due to his Barakah (blessing), I had the privilege of seeing Rasūlullāh 🌸 in my dream for the first time.

One day, he paused and related a story. There was a pious, poor student in a Dārul Uloom in Gujarat. He never disclosed his needs to anyone. He was once in a dire need and sought Allāh's 🌸 help.

The next day, a pious wealthy person came to the Madrasah's office and enquired about the student. The student was called over and the pious person handed him a bag of money and said Rasūlullāh 🌼 came in my dream and instructed me to give you this amount.

Qāri Sāhib 🌼 went on to say that this shows that our A'māl (deeds) are presented to Rasūlullāh 🌼. He also worries about us and prays for us. I had an Ajeeb (strange) feeling of love for Rasūlullāh 🌼. Tears came in my eyes and I wished that Rasūlullāh 🌼 would pray for me or I could see him in a dream. When I went to sleep that night, I did see him.

I saw that we were in a Masjid. Someone said Rasūlullāh's 🌼 Janāzah is coming. There were plenty of people and a lot of noise. The Janāzah was brought and placed in the courtyard of the Masjid. His Chādar Mubārak (blessed cloak) was removed. He stood up and began to walk. I rushed to him, embraced him and kissed his blessed hand. I asked for some advice and I remember him saying "Know that this is just a dream." There was a dispute between two parties and he said, "I am going there to make peace between both parties."

I must have related the dream to Qāri Sāhib 🌼. I also told Shaykh Yūnus Sāhib later on, who said, "Relate it to Yūsuf, he will give a good Ta'beer (interpretation)."

When our Hadhrat (Shaykh Yūsuf Motāla Sāhib) arrived in Saharanpūr (for the last 10 days), I related the dream to him and he said there are Fitnahs surrounding us and Rasūlullāh 🌸 is worried about them. As for the words of advice, they are to keep your feet on the ground so that you do not start boasting to people about this dream, it is just a dream.

During the Dārul Uloom I'tikāf, (I think it was 1989) Qāri Sāhib 🌸 would lead Qiyāmul Layl in his Mu'takaf. I would be his Sāmi' (listener). I would have to correct his mistakes. He hardly made any mistakes. He had a beautiful voice and a beautiful tune. Sometimes, I would copy his tune.

Qāri Sāhib 🌸 was very punctual; a man of principal. He was very punctual of his Ma'moolāt (daily prescribed readings). He was very adhering to Miswāk. His son, Qāri Fārūq Sāhib told me that he went to the dentist for the first time at the age of 70. The dentist was amazed that all his teeth were healthy. He asked him how he managed to keep them so healthy. Qāri Sāhib 🌸 took a Miswāk out of his pocket, showed him and said, "I brush my teeth with this 5 times a day."

Some sayings of Qāri Ismāeel Sāhib 🌸, related by Maulāna Khaleel Qāzi Sāhib,

"One should make Du'ā that his end is upon Imān, even though his body is torn into pieces he will remain valuable."

"When a scholar is given a position, he becomes famous."

"Simplicity is a sign of Imān."

"Great in this world is he who has power and position."

"If Allāh 🕸 wishes to grace someone, He is not dependant upon physical features. Uwais Qarni 🕸 was distant but became close and Abu Jahl was close but became distant."

May Allāh 🕸 shower immense Rahmah (mercy) upon Hadhrat Qāri Sāhib. Āmeen.

The Apple Tree and the Little Boy

A long time ago, there was a huge apple tree. A little boy loved to come and play around it every day. He climbed to the treetop, ate the apples and took a nap under the shadow. He loved the tree and the tree loved to play with him.

Time went by and the little boy had grown up. He no longer played around the tree every day.

One day, the boy came back to the tree and he looked sad.

"Come and play with me," the tree asked the boy.

"I am no longer a child, I do not play around trees anymore," the boy replied. "I want toys. I need money to buy them."

The tree said, "Sorry, but I do not have money, but you can pick all my apples and sell them, so you will have money."

The boy was so excited. He grabbed all the apples on the tree and left happily. The boy never came back after he picked the apples. The tree was sad.

One day, the boy who now turned into a man, returned and the tree was excited.

"Come and play with me," the tree said.
The man replied, "I do not have time to play. I have to work for my family. We need a house for shelter. Can you help me?"

The tree said, "Sorry, I do not have any house, but you can chop off my branches to build your house."

So the man cut all the branches of the tree and left happily. The tree was glad to see him happy but the man never came back. The tree was again lonely and sad.

One hot summer day, the man returned and the tree was delighted."Come and play with me!" the tree said.

"I am getting old. I want to go sailing to relax myself. Can you give me a boat?" said the man.

The tree replied, "Use my trunk to build your boat. You can sail far away and be happy."

So the man cut the tree trunk to make a boat. He went sailing and did not show up for a long time.

Finally, the man returned after many years.

"Sorry, my boy, but I do not have anything for you anymore. No more apples for you," the tree said.

"No problem, I do not have any teeth to bite," the man replied. The tree said, "No more trunk for you to climb on."

"I am too old for that now," the man said.

"I really cannot give you anything. The only thing left is my dying roots," the tree said with tears.

"I do not need much now, just a place to rest. I am tired after all these years," the man replied.

"Good! Old tree roots are the best place to lean on and rest. Come sit down with me and rest." The man sat down and the tree was glad and smiled with tears.

This is the story of everyone. The tree is like our parents. When we were young, we loved to play with our mum and dad. When we grow up, we leave them; only come to them when we need something or when we are in trouble. No matter what, parents will always be there and give everything they could just to make us happy. You may think the boy is cruel to the tree, but that is how all of us treat our parents. We take them for granted; we do not appreciate all they do for us, until it is too late.

Moral

Treat your parents with loving car, for you will know their value, when you see their empty chair. We never know the love of our parents for us until we have become parents ourselves.

Shaytān Circulates in You!!

Sayyidah Safiyyah Bint Huyai 🌸, the wife of the Holy Prophet 🌸 and the Mother of the Believers said, "I came to visit the Prophet 🌸 while he was in the state of Itikāf (seclusion in the Masjid). After having talked to him, I got up to return. The Prophet 🌸 also got up with me and accompanied me a part of the way.

At that moment two Ansāri men passed by. When they saw him, they quickened their pace. The Prophet 🌸 said to them, 'Do not hurry. She is Safiyyah, daughter of Huyai, my wife.' They said, 'Subhān-Allāh (Allāh 🌸 is free from imperfection)! O Messenger of Allāh 🌸! (You are far away from any suspicion).' The Messenger of Allāh 🌸 replied, 'Shaytān circulates in a person like blood. I apprehended lest Shaytān should drop some evil thought in your minds.'" [Bukhāri]

Even a passing thought of something undesirable about the Prophet 🌸 is dangerous for Imān (faith). In order to prevent any evil suspicions arising, the Prophet 🌸 stopped the two Companions and explained to them the situation. This was done lest Shaytān creates some doubt in the minds of the two Companions.

The conclusion from this Hadeeth is that if at any time, there is a chance that your actions will allow somebody to question your uprightness, then it is necessary to give an explanation to clarify the situation. This is particularly important for Ulama (scholars) who should remain aloof from such occasions and places that might induce people to start doubting their integrity and piety. This hap-

63

pens because Shaytān is always trying to sow discord between people.

On the other hand, one should not jump to evil conclusions regarding others, but always give them the benefit of the doubt. The Prophet ﷺ advisedto make seventy excuses for your Muslim brother or sister before you accuse him or her of anything. Do we even try to come up with even one excuse, before rushing to pass an unfavourable judgement?

Four Useful Actions

Rasūlullāh ﷺ said, "Any action which is void of the remembrance of Allāh ﷻ is Lahw (futile) except for four actions.

1) Walking between two targets, i.e. practicing with a bow and arrow/spear.

2) Training ones horse.

3) Playing with ones wife.

4) Learning how to swim.

Dangers of Being Praised

For many Muslims involved in Da'wah work or Islamic activities, one of the biggest struggles they face is praise and fame from their communities and peers. It is the nature of humans to praise what they see of people, but we are taught in our Deen that too much praise can harm a person.

The Prophet ﷺ heard a man praising another and he responded to him, "May Allāh's ﷻ mercy be upon you! You have cut the neck of your friend." [Bukhāri]

My teacher used to say, "Praise is poison," because of how it can ruin a good intention into a corrupt one. When we are constantly praised, our weak souls, begin to rely and covet this praise, so good deeds are then done solely to hear those words of praise. A person's Nafs may rely so much on this praise that they begin seeking it for what they did not do. Allāh ﷻ describes in the Qur'an,

$$\text{لَا تَحْسَبَنَّ الَّذِيْنَ يَفْرَحُوْنَ بِمَا أَتَوْا وَّيُحِبُّوْنَ أَنْ يُّحْمَدُوْا بِمَا لَمْ يَفْعَلُوْا فَلَا تَحْسَبَنَّهُمْ بِمَفَازَةٍ مِّنَ الْعَذَابِ}$$

"Never think that those people are safe from punishment who boast about what they do and enjoy to be praised for what they did not do..." (3:188)

The scholars and righteous of the past would find ways to keep this praise away from themselves and remind those around them to not over praise others. This is why we find many narrations where they humiliate or speak lowly of themselves to keep their Nafs in check.

There is a supplication which was not taught to us by the Prophet ﷺ, but it is one that his best friend, Abū Bakr ؓ would make after being praised (some narrations state that it was a Du'ā of Ali ؓ).

It is reported that he would say,

اللّٰهُمَّ اجْعَلْنِيْ خَيْرًا مِّمَّا يَظُنُّوْنَ وَاغْفِرْ لِيْ مَا لَا يَعْلَمُوْنَ وَلَا تُؤَاخِذْنِيْ بِمَا يَقُوْلُوْنَ

O Allāh ﷻ, make me better than what they think of me, forgive me for what they do not know about me and do not take me to account for what they say about me.

Analysis of Selected Words

يَظُنُّوْنَ – Dhann is supposition. Notice here that Abū Bakr ؓ did not say, "ya'lamoon", "what they know" but rather, he used Ya-dhunnūn— "what they think about me." He is showing us through the use of this word that what people think is not always true and supposition can never equate to actual knowledge.

تُؤَاخِذْنِيْ - ākhadha means to reproach or blame someone. It means to hold someone accountable for something. Sayyidunā Abū Bakr ؓ is asking that he not be held accountable for what is said about him, because it is not in his control.

Points of Benefit,

Being praised is something that even great personalities struggle with. Sayyidunā Abū Bakr ☝ was the giant of this Ummah, the greatest man after the Prophets, yet he struggled with hearing the praises of others. Struggling with praises does not mean you are weak, rather it means you are human. Be careful in overpraising others. Sometimes we over-exaggerate in praising people and this only hurts the person more.

The Prophet ﷺ said, "You are cutting the neck of your brother" in other words, you may think you are benefiting the person but it may only be hurting them more.

It is important to be balanced when praising others. The Prophet ﷺ said, "If it is necessary for any of you to praise someone, then he should say, 'I think that he is so-and-so', if he really thinks that he is such. Allāh ﷻ is the One Who will take his account (as He knows his reality) and none can sanctify anyone before Allāh ﷻ." [Bukhāri].

Once a man was praised by another, so he asked him, "Have you seen me while I was angry and found me forbearing?" The man who praised him said no. He then asked, "Have you travelled with me and saw that I had good character (during travels)?" He said no. Then he asked, "Have you found me trustworthy with regards to fulfilling the trusts?" He said no. The man concluded, "Then it is not allowed for you to praise someone if you have not seen his behaviour with regards to these situations."

Make Du'ā for those who are faced with popularity, fame and praise. It is a great inner struggle for them.

Being praised for an action you did secretly for the sake of Allāh ﷻ is a good thing. It was said to Allāh's Messenger ﷺ, "What is your opinion about the person who has done good deeds and the people praise him?" He said, "It is glad tidings for a believer (which he has received in this world)." [Muslim]

This is not the same as someone acting out due to seeking praise or changing their deeds afterward for praise, but this is when someone is praised for what they have already done such as people finding out that they were feeding the poor or praying during the night. If you are praised, then be careful not to let praise and self admiration overcome you. Praise makes people arrogant and content with their deeds so they do not worship or do good as much because they are happy with their situation.

Some Sayings of the Salaf (Pious Predecessors) Regarding Praise/Fame,

Al-Kuraybi ﷺ said, "They used to prefer that a man hide his righteous deeds (to the extent) that his wife or anyone else would not be aware of it." (As-Siyar, 9/349)

Abū Hāzim ﷺ said, "Hide your good deeds more than you hide your bad deeds." (Al-Musannaf, 7/195)

Fudayl Ibn 'Iyād ﷺ said, "Whosoever is saddened by loneliness and feels tranquil around the people is not safe from Riyā (showing off)." (As-Siyar, 8/436)

Sa'eed Ibnul Haddād ﷺ said, "Nothing hinders from the path of Allāh ﷻ like seeking praise and status." (As-Siyar, 14/214)

Sufyān Ath-Thawri ﷺ said, "Safety is that you do not desire to be known." (As-Siyar, 7,257)

Bishr Ibnul-Hārith ﷺ said, "The (person) that loves fame has not feared Allāh ﷻ. Do not act in order to be mentioned and hide your good deeds like you hide your bad ones." (As-Siyar, 10/476)

May Allāh ﷻ make us among the sincere ones and may He purify our hearts from seeking praise and being affected by it. Āmeen.

Wake Up! Open Your Eyes!

How many times do we feel the need to fit in to the society, doing what everyone else does just so people do not take a second look at us? We fear the piercing stares and gossip of the average human being so much that we often restrict ourselves to only thinking average thoughts. We go to work everyday hoping our lives change to something better but we still act the same way we did yesterday.

Wake Up! Open Your Eyes!

You are beyond average; you have dreams, aspirations and the imagination to conquer the world, yet you are still on your bed in the morning thinking how you are going to conform to the society you live in; wearing the same clothes, same shoes, same speech and the same mentality.

What has the society you live in done for you? Killing innocent people all around the world, raping children and women, lying, cheating, Zina, bullying, torturing, spying yet you still wish to shackle your thoughts and your mind to think average thoughts like every average human being walking on this earth?

Do not be afraid to be different, do not be afraid to stand out and do not be afraid to be who you are, because the society you live in just wants you to be who they are. Like a teacher will teach his students only what he knows, not knowing that the students may have more potential than him. The teacher's fear is that his students may become better than him. In the similar manner, the society fears every individual with the mind to do good and bring about changes to the corrupted society that the leaders of today have created.

Think different. Think positive. Think Islām. Islām came as something strange to the world and it will always be strange to the world, because the world is too corrupted to accept the pure nature of Islām as anything other than strange. So glad tidings to the strangers!

Smart and Genius

Anyone who wants a second wife has to be as smart as this guy;

A man from the tribe of Banū Nawfal Ibn 'Abd Manāf married a second wife who was fair and pretty. Umm Mahjan, his first wife, who was not as pretty, was upset when she heard the news. Jealousy and disappointment drove her to confront her husband, but he explained,

"By Allāh ﷻ, Umm Mahjan, there is no need to guard me anymore. I am an old man. You too are old and there is no need for me to be jealous over you. Nobody can be more honoured in my sight than you; neither does anybody enjoy a greater right over me than you. I, therefore advise you to accept my decision and avoid bad thoughts from taking hold of you."

These words pleased her and she felt comfortable. A few days later, he said to her, "Wouldn't you like to live together with my new wife? I think it would create harmony between us. Further, it will be a means of systematic organisation within our home and it will prevent outsiders from making nasty remarks against us."

She agreed and he gave her a Dinār, saying, "I dislike your co-wife seeking superiority over you simply because she sees you enjoying some speciality. Take this and prepare some special gift which you can give to her tomorrow when we meet."

He then approached his new wife and said, "I intend to unite you with Umm Mahjan tomorrow. She wants to honour you and I dislike her making any attempt to be superior than you simply because you enjoy some speciality. Take this Dinār and purchase for her a gift so that she does not regard you with scepticism. However, do not mention anything to her about the Dinār."

He then approached a trusted friend and sought his assistance, "I have arranged for my new wife to meet with Umm Mahjan tomorrow. I would like you to visit us at breakfast, at which time I will insist that you join us. When we are done with the meal, you should ask me which wife I hold dearer. I will express my displeasure at the question, following which, you should insist upon oath that I answer you."

The next morning, his new wife visited Umm Mahjan and his friend came around as agreed. After they had eaten, his friend turned to him and asked, "Which of your two wives do you love more?"

He replied, "Subhān-Allāh! Do you dare ask a question of this nature while both my wives are listening to our discussion. This is a grave question indeed."

When his friend insisted on an answer, he declared, "I love that wife who was given one Dinār. I will not utter a word more than this."

Each of the two wives chuckled in pleasure, thinking that she was the one alluded to.

Common Sense

Today we mourn the passing of a beloved old friend, Common Sense, who has been with us for many years. No one knows for sure how old he was, since his birth records were long ago lost in bureaucratic red tape.

He will be remembered as having cultivated such valuable lessons as,

- Knowing when to come in out of the rain;
- Why the early bird gets the worm;
- Life is not always fair; and
- Maybe it was my fault.

Common Sense lived by simple, sound, financial policies (do not spend more than you can earn) and reliable strategies (adults, not children, are in charge). His health began to deteriorate rapidly when well-intentioned but overbearing regulations were set in place.

Reports of a 6-year-old boy charged with sexual harassment for kissing a classmate, teens suspended from school for using mouthwash after lunch and a teacher fired for reprimanding an unruly student only worsened his condition.

Common Sense lost ground when parents attacked teachers for doing the job that they themselves had failed to do in disciplining their unruly children. It declined even further when schools were required to get parental consent to administer sun lotion or an aspirin to a student but could not inform parents when a student became pregnant and wanted to have an abortion.

Common Sense lost the will to live as the places of worship became businesses and criminals received better treatment than their victims. Common Sense took a beating when you could not defend yourself from a burglar in your own home and the burglar could sue you for assault.

Common Sense finally gave up the will to live after a woman failed to realise that a steaming cup of coffee was hot. She spilled a little in her lap and was promptly awarded a huge settlement.

Common Sense was preceded in death by his parents, Truth and Trust, by his wife, Discretion, by his daughter, Responsibility, and by his son, Reason.

He is survived by his 4 stepbrothers,

- I Know My Rights,
- I Want It Now,
- Someone Else Is To Blame, and
- I am A Victim.

Not many attended his funeral because so few realised he was gone!!!

Shaykh Zakariyyah ﷺ on the Ahlul-Hadeeth

In Volume 5 of his autobiography, "Āp Beeti," Shaykhul Hadeeth Maulāna Muhammad Zakariyyah Kandhlawi ﷺ himself writes,

In both Deoband and Saharanpūr, there were many Ahlul-Hadeeth students, but they never disclosed their adherence to the Ahlul-Hadeeth. I told them not to hide their Madhab from me. They could come to my house at any time to discuss their problems.

Some students (may Allāh ﷻ reward them) came to me to be connected in Bai'ah. Some people suggested that I should demand them to stop 'Raf-ul-Yadayn' (raising the hands), 'Āmeen-Bil-Jahr' (saying Āmeen audibly) etc., but I told them, "You people are doing those thing in your earnest desire to implement Rasūlullāh's ﷺ commands and practices. How can I ever prohibit you from doing so?"

Subhān-Allāh, our Akābir (elders) in general were so moderate and did not condemn people for interpreting Islām a different way. Indeed, as long as someone is trying to satisfy Allāh ﷻ through his actions, he should not be stopped or criticised, as long as his action are not against Shari'ah, do not harm other people or fall in the category of Bid'ah (innovations).

A few pages later, Shaykhul Hadeeth Maulāna Zakariyyah Sāhib

🕮 writes down his thoughts in general about the Ahlul Hadeeth and us."

I have no enmity with any Ahlul Hadeeth scholars, so long as they do not use any insulting or degrading words against our Imāms. In my mind, 'Shari'at' is only that which is contained in Allāh's 🕮 word and the words and practices of His Messenger 🕮. However, in acting on the Hadeeth and in cross examining the Hadeeth, the research of the Imāms is much more preferable to the research of a novice like myself. Also, the era of the Imāms was nearer to the era of the scholars of Hadeeth. For this reason, the verdict of the Imāms are more acceptable in the rejection and acceptance of Hadeeth than even the verdict of Muhaddithoon and our research.

Imām Ahmad Ibn Hanbal 🕮 is Imām Bukhāri's 🕮 most noted teacher, while Imām Ahmad 🕮 is Imām Shāfi'ee's 🕮 most prominent student. Imām Shāfi'ee 🕮 again, is the most famous student of Imām Mālik 🕮. Imām Shāfi'ee 🕮 is on record as having said that he became a jurist after studying the books of Imām Muhammad Ibn Hasan Ash-Shaybāni 🕮, the famous student of Imām Abū Haneefah 🕮. Furthermore, there are twenty two chains of transmission of Hadeeth in Bukhāri Shareef, each consisting of three people only, leading up to Rasūlullāh 🕮. Of these twenty two, twenty of them contain transmitters who are either students of Imām Abū Haneefah 🕮 or students of his students. As for us of this era, we are like monkeys who sit down with a piece of ginger and then call themselves green-grocers.

Imagine…

Imagine leaving your home.
Imagine being told to run.

Imagine knowing that your enemy will loot your possessions.

Imagine having to hide your women from the lusts of animals.

Imagine cutting your daughter's hair so short that she looks like a boy in order to keep attention away from her.

Imagine being stripped naked in front of your family.

Imagine your children being slapped in front of you. and you could not do anything.

Imagine telling your family to sleep through the pain of hunger. and watching them cry to sleep.

Imagine soldiers telling you that they will let you pass if they can spend some time with your wife or your daughter.

Imagine having to steal food from your starving neighbours just to feed your own family.

Imagine wishing death for your children just to put them out of their misery.

Then imagine knowing.. that your brothers and sisters saw your plight and did nothing!!

Be someone that does something!

What to do After Ramadhān

Now that we come to the end of Ramadhān, the big question is, What to do?

Did we go through all the spiritual exercises in Ramadhān in order that we may have the freedom to indulge on Eid day, in all types of immoral, shameless and indecent entertainment and amusement?

Did we restrain ourselves from Halāl food, drinks and other pleasures from dawn to sunset throughout Ramadhān, so that we may return with renewed vigour to gambling, drinking, adultery and fornication?

Will the spirit of tolerance, mercy, patience, charity, sympathy and the nurtured quality of piety and Allāh-Consciousness be still evident or will these noble qualities be shelved until the dawn of the next Ramadhān?

Will the Masājid which were filled on most nights in Ramadhān remain the same or will they become empty, wondering where the faithful have gone?

Our life-styles after Ramadhān will show whether we used the month to bring about a total reformation within ourselves or whether we wasted the valuable opportunity.

Visa of Life

Strange is the Visa of life.
It can be cancelled at anytime.
The duration of its validity is unknown,
and its Extension too, is impossible.
(*Shaykh Yūnus Patel Sāhib, South Africa*)

The Power of Making Istighfār

During his old age, while Imām Ahmad ﷺ was travelling, he stopped by a town. After the prayers, he wanted to stay for the night in the Masjid yard because he did not know anyone in the town. Owing to his humility, he had not introduced himself to anyone thinking that if he did, he would be welcomed by many people. Failing to recognize Imām Ahmad Ibn Hanbal ﷺ, the caretaker of the Masjid refused to let him stay in the Masjid. As Imām Ahmad ﷺ was quite old, the caretaker had to drag him out of the Masjid.

On seeing this, a baker from a nearby place felt pity for this man (Imām Ahmad ﷺ) and offered to be his host for the night. During his stay with the baker, Imām Ahmad ﷺ observed that the baker would constantly recite Istighfār (seeking forgiveness from Allāh ﷻ).

Imām Ahmad ﷺ asked the baker if the constant practice of Istighfār had any effect on him.

The baker responded by telling Imām Ahmad ﷺ that Allāh ﷻ had accepted all of his Du'ās (supplications), except one. When he asked him what Du'ā it was that had not been accepted, the baker replied that he had been asking Allāh ﷻ to provide him the privilege to meet the famous scholar Imām Ahmad Ibn Hanbal ﷺ.

On this, Imām Ahmad Ibn Hanbal ﷺ said that Allāh ﷻ had not only listened to his Du'ā, but He had dragged him onto his (the baker's) doorstep!

[Summarized from Al-Jumuah magazine, vol 19, issue 7]

Subhān-Allāh! Imagine, if in our daily routines we just repeated 'Astaghfirrullāh,' Allāh ﷻ will open ways for us and accept our Du'ās readily.

Success in this World and the Hereafter

In order to be successful in this world and the Hereafter remember three points.

1) Safeguard your tongue.
2) Let your house be sufficient (i.e. be content on what you have and remain within your home to save yourself from sinning like sin of eyes etc.)
3) Cry over your sins.

To further enhance your spirituality, act upon the following two points:

1) Take what is clear and beneficial.
2) Leave that which is doubtful.

In order to safeguard yourself from backbiting, slandering, malice etc. go through the triple filter test.

1) Is it true?
2) Is there any goodness in it?
3) Is it beneficial for me or not?

This test has proven to work and benefited many people.

(Shaykh Mufti Saiful Islām)

The Reality of Ego and Pride

Once, a pious old man encountered a youngster who was walking towards him with his chest out and head held high. As he walked by the pious man, he bumped into him, nudging him to the side. The pious man said to the youngster in a soft voice, "My son, please do not walk like that."

With a furious and arrogant voice the youngster yelled out,

"What!? Do you know who I am, old man!?"

The pious man replied calmly, "Yes my son, I know exactly who you are. Your beginning was from an impure semen. your ending will become a decomposed body and right now, you are carrying urine and excretion inside you."

In reality, a person showing pride and arrogance is nothing but one whose beginning was an impure semen and whose ending will become a decomposed body and at that moment that same body is carrying urine and excretion inside.

Allāh ﷻ dislikes pride in a person. It is a spiritual illness that we need to remove from ourselves. One of the most effective methods is remembering Allāh ﷻ abundantly. Remember, pride is what got Shaytān expelled from Jannah and which turned him from an Ābid (worshipper) to Ar-Rajeem (the rejected one).

(Shaykh Mufti Saiful Islām)

Golden Advice of Luqmān عليه السلام

(Shaykh Mufti Saiful Islām)

1) When you are in Ibādah take care of your heart (i.e. sincerity and devotion is incumbent during any form of worship).

2) When you are in a gathering, take care of your tongue (i.e. from backbiting, slandering, taunting , futile talk). This includes social networking, so verify information before circulating.

In order to safeguard yourself from backbiting, slandering, taunting etc. go through the Triple Filter Test.
a) Is it true?
b) Is there any goodness in it?
c) Is it beneficial for me or not?

3) When you are in someone's house safeguard your eyes and lower your gaze.

4) When you are eating, consume only Halāl food for it gives us strength to carry out good deeds.

5) Remember Allāh ﷻ abundantly even though people may start calling you a mad man.

6) Never forget death

جُمُوۡدُ الۡعَيۡنِ مِنۡ قَسۡوَةِ الۡقَلۡبِ

وَقَسۡوَةُ الۡقَلۡبِ مِنۡ كَثۡرَةِ الذُّنُوۡبِ

وَكَثْرَةُ الذُّنُوبِ مِنْ نِسْيَانِ الْمَوْتِ

وَنِسْيَانُ الْمَوْتِ مِنْ طُوْلِ الْأَمَلِ

وَطُوْلُ الْأَمَلِ مِنْ حُبِّ الدُّنْيَا

وَحُبُّ الدُّنْيَا رَأْسُ كُلِّ خَطِيْئَةٍ

The lack of tears is the result of hard-heartedness;
Hard-heartedness is caused due to excessive sinning;
Excessive sins are the result of forgetting death;
Forgetting death is due to lengthy desires;
Lengthy desires are caused because of attachment to the world;
And love of the world is the root of all evils.

7) If you do good for someone, forget about it i.e. do not remind them and do not boast about it.

8) If someone does evil to you, forget about it. Do not retaliate and forgive the person.

May Allāh ﷻ give us the ability to inculcate such qualities in our lives. Āmeen.

Allāh's ﷻ Anger and Ways of Remedy

Question,

The Religious Scholars (Ulamā) are requested to shed light upon the factors behind the distress and suffering of Muslims all over the world. Muslims are facing riots and massacres at many places, why is this?

Answer,

There are several reasons for this sad state of affairs in the Ummah. Among the more prominent ones are the following,

1. Lack of Imān-e-Kāmil (true faith in Allāh ﷻ)
2. Increased disobedience towards Him.
3. Increased cowardice among us.
4. Love of the materialistic world [Hubb-e-Dunya wal Māl].
5. Open disobedience of the Sunnah of Rasūlullāh ﷺ.
6. Following our own innovated [bid'ah] practices and customs.
7. Neglecting the rights of Allāh ﷻ [Huqūq-Allāh] and the rights of creation [Huqūq-ul-Ibād].
8. Our complete ingratitude towards the innumerable blessings showered upon us by our Benefactor, despite being totally unworthy of these blessings.
9. Disregard for the selfless advice given to us by our noble Ulamā in relation to our religion.

Allāh ﷻ sums up the reasons for our suffering in the Qur'ān,

وَمَا أَصَابَكُم مِّن مُّصِيبَةٍ فَبِمَا كَسَبَتْ أَيْدِيكُمْ وَيَعْفُوا عَن كَثِيرٍ

"The misfortunes that afflict you are a result of the (evil) actions you earn and Allāh pardons great deal."(42:30)

A further elaboration on this point is found in the Qur'ān,

"ظَهَرَ الْفَسَادُ فِي الْبَرِّ وَالْبَحْرِ بِمَا كَسَبَتْ أَيْدِي النَّاسِ لِيُذِيقَهُم بَعْضَ الَّذِي عَمِلُوا لَعَلَّهُمْ يَرْجِعُونَ

"Corruption has appeared on land and at sea because of the (evil) actions of man and so that Allāh may let them taste of some of their actions, so that they may turn back." (30:41)

Punishments for Certain Types of Sins

Indulging in disobedience and committing sins angers Allāh ﷻ, but certain sins are such that, if committed, will invite a very swift and severe punishment.

Among these types of sins are,

1. Unjust decision-making and the breaking of pledges - will cause the imposition of tyrannical rule.
2. Short-weighing and short-measuring by traders will cause the punishment of famine, inflation and oppression.
3. Widespread betrayal of trust will cause the imposition of tyrant rulers.
4. Fearing death and inclining towards Dunya (materialism) will result in timidity and fear among the faithful. (Jazā-ul-A'māl).

The Companion, Sayyidunā Thawbān ؓ narrated that the Prophet ﷺ said, "A period will come when the enemies will be calling one another against you, for annexing the nations of the believers, just like how people call one another for eating food when it has been prepared. "

Someone then asked as to whether the Muslims will be few in number (at that time)? Rasūlullāh ﷺ replied, "No, you will be large in numbers, but you will be as feeble as the froth of the flood water. Allāh ﷻ will extract from the hearts of your enemies (their) awe of you and place weakness into your hearts." The person asked, "What will this weakness be?" He replied, "Love of the world and dislike of death." [Abū Dāwood]

Other titles from JKN Publications

Your Questions Answered

An outstanding book written by Shaykh Mufti Saiful Islām. A very comprehensive yet simple Fatāwa book and a source of guidance that reaches out to a wider audience i.e. the English speaking Muslims. The reader will benefit from the various answers to questions based on the Laws of Islām relating to the beliefs of Islām, knowledge, Sunnah, pillars of Islām, marriage, divorce and contemporary issues.

UK RRP, £7.50

Hadeeth for Beginners

A concise Hadeeth book with various Ahādeeth that relate to basic Ibādāh and moral etiquettes in Islām accessible to a wider readership. Each Hadeeth has been presented with the Arabic text, its translation and commentary to enlighten the reader, its meaning and application in day-to-day life.

UK RRP, £3.00

Du'ā for Beginners

This book contains basic Du'ās which every Muslim should recite on a daily basis. Highly recommended to young children and adults studying at Islamic schools and Madrasahs so that one may cherish the beautiful treasure of supplications of our beloved Prophet ﷺ in one's daily life, which will ultimately bring peace and happiness in both worlds, Inshā-Allāh.

UK RRP, £2.00

How well do you know Islām?

An exciting educational book which contains 300 multiple questions and answers to help you increase your knowledge on Islām! Ideal for the whole family, especially children and adult students to learn new knowledge in an enjoyable way and cherish the treasures of knowledge that you will acquire from this book. A very beneficial tool for educational syllabus.

UK RRP, £3.00

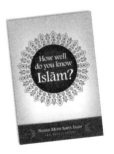

Treasures of the Holy Qur'ān

This book entitled "Treasures of the Holy Qur'ān" has been compiled to create a stronger bond between the Holy Qur'ān and the readers. It mentions the different virtues of Sūrahs and verses from the Holy Qur'ān with the hope that the readers will increase their zeal and enthusiasm to recite and inculcate the teachings of the Holy Qur'ān into their daily lives.

UK RRP, £3.00

Other titles from JKN PUBLICATIONS

Marriage - A Complete Solution
Islām regards marriage as a great act of worship. This book has been designed to provide the fundamental teachings and guidelines of all what relates to the marital life in a simplified English language. It encapsulates in a nutshell all the marriage laws mentioned in many of the main reference books in order to facilitate their understanding and implementation.

UK RRP, £5.00

Pearls of Luqmān
This book is a comprehensive commentary of Sūrah Luqmān, written beautifully by Shaykh Mufti Saiful Islām. It offers the reader with an enquiring mind, abundance of advice, guidance, counselling and wisdom.

The reader will be enlightened by many wonderful topics and anecdotes mentioned in this book, which will create a greater understanding of the Holy Qur'ān and its wisdom. The book highlights some of the wise sayings and words of advice Luqmān ﷺ gave to his son.

UK RRP, £3.00

Arabic Grammar for Beginners
This book is a study of Arabic Grammar based on the subject of Nahw (Syntax) in a simplified English format. If a student studies this book thoroughly, he/she will develop a very good foundation in this field, Inshā-Allāh. Many books have been written on this subject in various languages such as Arabic, Persian and Urdu. However, in this day and age there is a growing demand for this subject to be available in English .

UK RRP, £3.00

A Gift to My Youngsters
This treasure filled book, is a collection of Islamic stories, morals and anecdotes from the life of our beloved Prophet ﷺ, his Companions ﷺ and the pious predecessors. The stories and anecdotes are based on moral and ethical values, which the reader will enjoy sharing with their peers, friends, families and loved ones.

"A Gift to My Youngsters" – is a wonderful gift presented to the readers personally, by the author himself, especially with the youngsters in mind. He has carefully selected stories and anecdotes containing beautiful morals, lessons and valuable knowledge and wisdom.

UK RRP, £5.00

Travel Companion
The beauty of this book is that it enables a person on any journey, small or distant or simply at home, to utilise their spare time to read and benefit from an exciting and vast collection of important and interesting Islamic topics and lessons. Written in simple and easy to read text, this book will immensely benefit both the newly interested person in Islām and the inquiring mind of a student expanding upon their existing knowledge. Inspiring reminders from the Holy Qur'ān and the blessed words of our beloved Prophet ﷺ beautifies each topic and will illuminate the heart of the reader.   **UK RRP, £5.00**

Pearls of Wisdom

Junaid Baghdādi ﷺ once said, "Allāh ﷻ strengthens through these Islamic stories the hearts of His friends, as proven from the Qur'anic verse,
"And all that We narrate unto you of the stories of the Messengers, so as to strengthen through it your heart." (11,120)
Mālik Ibn Dinār ﷺ stated that such stories are gifts from Paradise. He also emphasised to narrate these stories as much as possible as they are gems and it is possible that an individual might find a truly rare and invaluable gem among them.   **UK RRP, £6.00**

Inspirations
This book contains a compilation of selected speeches delivered by Shaykh Mufti Saiful Islam on a variety of topics such as the Holy Qur'ān, Nikāh and eating Halāl. Having previously been compiled in separate booklets, it was decided that the transcripts be gathered together in one book for the benefit of the reader. In addition to this, we have included in this book, further speeches which have not yet been printed.

UK RRP, £6.00

Gift to my Sisters

A thought provoking compilation of very interesting articles including real life stories of pious predecessors, imaginative illustrations and much more. All designed to influence and motivate mothers, sisters, wives and daughters towards an ideal Islamic lifestyle. A lifestyle referred to by our Creator, Allāh ﷻ in the Holy Qur'ān as the means to salvation and ultimate success.

UK RRP, £6.00

Gift to my Brothers
A thought provoking compilation of very interesting articles including real life stories of pious predecessors, imaginative illustrations, medical advices on intoxicants and rehabilitation and much more. All designed to influence and motivate fathers, brothers, husbands and sons towards an ideal Islamic lifestyle. A lifestyle referred to by our Creator, Allāh ﷻ in the Holy Qur'ān as the means to salvation and ultimate success.

UK RRP, £5.00

Heroes of Islām

"In the narratives there is certainly a lesson for people of intelligence (understanding)." (12,111)

A fine blend of Islamic personalities who have been recognised for leaving a lasting mark in the hearts and minds of people.

A distinguishing feature of this book is that the author has selected not only some of the most world and historically famous renowned scholars but also these lesser known and a few who have simply left behind a valuable piece of advice to their nearest and dearest. **UK RRP, £5.00**

Ask a Mufti (3 volumes)

Muslims in every generation have confronted different kinds of challenges. In-spite of that, Islām produced such luminary Ulamā who confronted and re-sponded to the challenges of their time to guide the Ummah to the straight path. "Ask A Mufti" is a comprehensive three volume fatwa book, based on the Hanafi School, covering a wide range of topics related to every aspect of human life such as belief, ritual worship, life after death and contemporary legal topics related to purity, commercial transaction, marriage, divorce, food, cosmetic, laws pertaining to women, Islamic medical ethics and much more.

Should I Follow a Madhab?

Taqleed or following one of the four legal schools is not a new phenomenon. Historically, scholars of great calibre and luminaries, each one being a specialist in his own right, were known to have adhered to one of the four legal schools. It is only in the previous century that a minority group emerged advocating a se-vere ban on following one of the four major schools.

This book endeavours to address the topic of Taqleed and elucidates why it is necessary to do Taqleed in this day and age. It will also, by the Divine Will of Allāh ﷻ dispel some of the confusion surrounding this topic. **UK RRP, £5.00**

Advice for the Students of Knowledge

Allāh ﷻ describes divine knowledge in the Holy Qur'ān as a 'Light'. Amongst the qualities of light are purity and guidance. The Holy Prophet ﷺ has clearly ex-plained this concept in many blessed Ahādeeth and has also taught us many supplications in which we ask for beneficial knowledge.

This book is a golden tool for every sincere student of knowledge wishing to mould his/her character and engrain those correct qualities in order to be wor-thy of receiving the great gift of Ilm from Allāh ﷻ. **UK RRP, £3.00**

Stories for Children

"Stories for Children" - is a wonderful gift presented to the readers personally, by the author himself, especially with the young children in mind. The stories are based on moral and ethical values, which the reader will enjoy sharing with their peers, friends, families and loved ones. The aim is to present to the children stories and incidents which contain moral lessons, in order to reform and correct their lives, according to the Holy Qur'ān and Sunnah.

UK RRP, £5.00